WHAT'S NEW, B.C.?

BY JOHNNY HART

A FAWCETT GOLD MEDAL BOOK

Fawcett Publications, Inc., Greenwich, Conn.

Member of American Book Publishers Council, Inc.

Fawcett Gold Medal Books by Johnny Hart:

50¢ Wherever Paperbacks Are Sold

SEE THE FUNNY, FUNNY WALL.

SEE JANE JUMP THE WALL.

JANE HAS DEFECTED.

SEE DICK PLAY.

SEE DICK WORK.

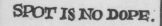

SEE SPOT WATCH
DICK WORK.

SPOT IS NO DOPE.

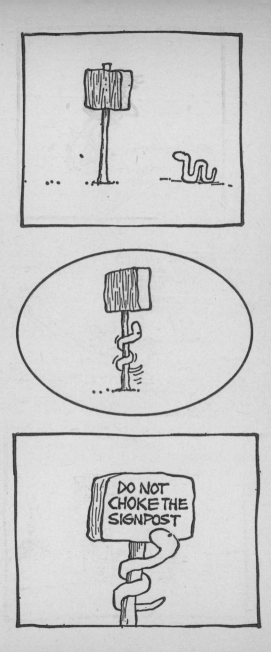

THE HECK WITH IDEAS.

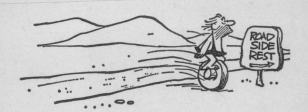

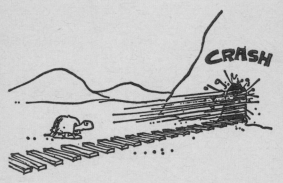

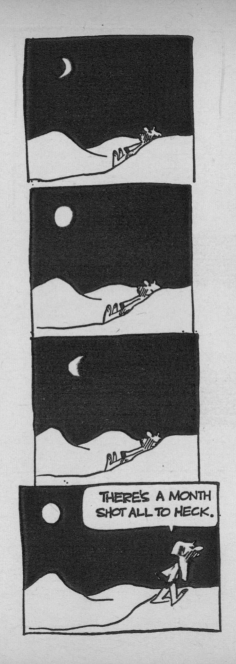

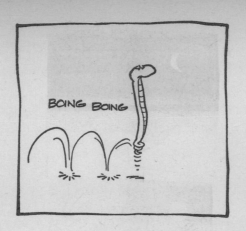

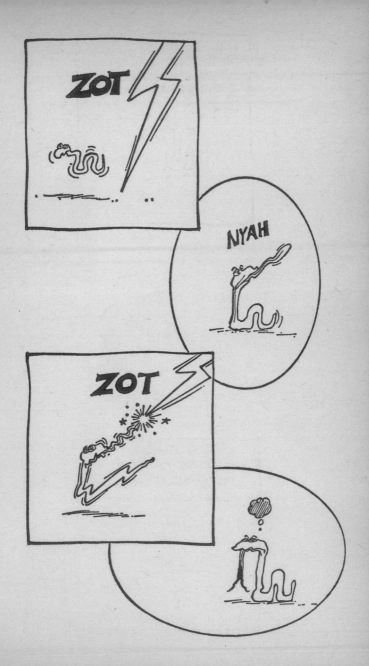

PICK

KWANG

IF HE THINKS I'M GOING TO PAY TO READ HIS BOOK; HE'S CRAZY.
SAY --THIS IS GOOD!
WOW --THIS IS TERRIFIC!

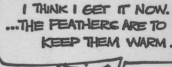

I THINK I GET IT NOW.
...THE FEATHERS ARE TO
KEEP THEM WARM.

KLUNK

NOW I KNOW
WHAT THEY MEAN
BY GOLF-WIDOW.

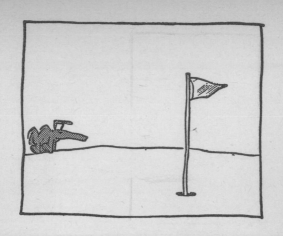

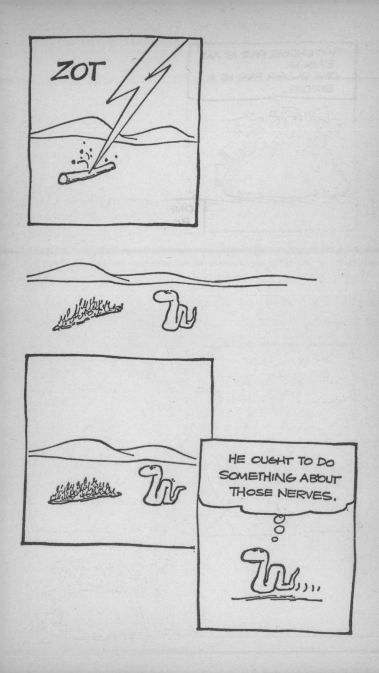

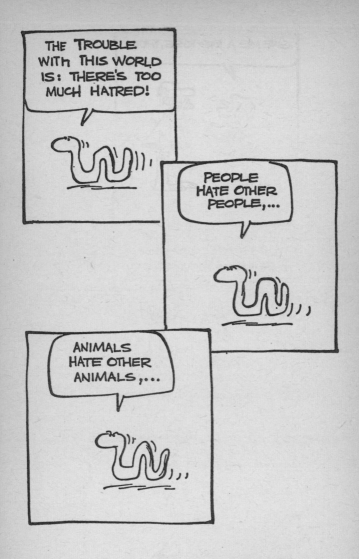

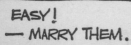

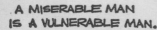

WHO IS YOUR LEGAL REPRESENTATIVE?
JVSTICE
I SHALL DEFEND MYSELF.
COURT ADJOURNED!
WHAP
JVSTICE
DIG UP A LAWYER, CHARLIE. THIS AIN'T NO 'B' MOVIE.
JVSTICE

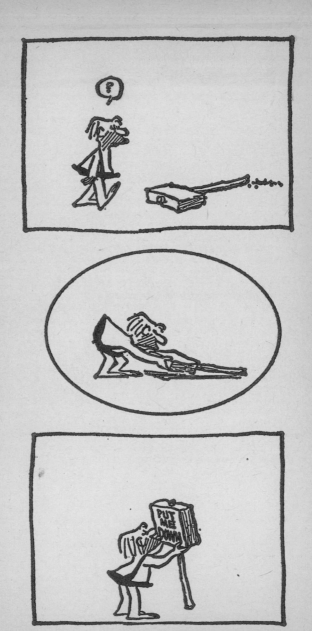